WILDLY AUSTIN

austin's landmark art

WILDLY AUSTIN SERIES / VOLUME 1

WILDLY AUSTIN™

austin's landmark art

BY VIKKI LOVING

PHOTOGRAPHY BY GREGG CESTARO

Wildly Austin Press

AUSTIN, TEXAS

First Edition

Printed by Capital Printing Co.
Austin, Texas

Front Cover Design by Nathan Procknow

Book Design by Leisha Israel, Blue Sky Media

Hardcover: ISBN# 0-9753990-1-2
Softcover: ISBN# 0-9753990-0-4

WILDLY AUSTIN PRESS
P.O. Box 161987, Austin, Texas 78714-1987

TO BROOKE AND LEA
and to the Belief in things
Greater than we can Wildly Imagine!

ACKNOWLEDGEMENTS

Thank you to all those who have encouraged me through the writing of this book:

Lea DuRard, Brooke Loving-Bagwell, Barry Coston, Dick and Eleanor Chote,
Madalene Allen, Jeff Nash, Kim and Austin Anderson, Melanie Williamson, Heidi Muth,
Bruce Bagwell, Pam Golightly, Sam Planta.
You have made this book greater than I could Wildly Imagine.

To Lisa Waggoner and Patti Halladay who supported me through their encouragement, loyalty and belief as well as keeping the business going while I took time for this project.

Gregg Cestaro for your talent and *wildly* artistic "eye" in taking the photographs.

Nathan Procknow for the front cover and website design.

Mitch Lobrovich for your creative input in the writing and editing of this text.

Margaret and Jim Talbot for their finishing touches in making this book its best.

Lori Carlson and Leisha Israel at Blue Sky Media and Capital Printing, Co.
for design and book production.

To my publishing consultant, Kathleen Niendorff, thank you for encouraging
and mentoring me through my first steps in the journey of publication.

And most of all, thanks to Austin— a city filled with people brave enough to follow their
hearts and dreams. Thanks to each of you for sharing so many stories with me and
allowing me in the process to find many new friends.

Introduction

At the end of the millennium, after spending sixteen years in Atlanta, I returned to my roots here in Austin. I discovered I'd forgotten just how unique and wonderful a city we had. I was also struck by how much Austin had changed in my absence. Some of my favorite places had disappeared, and others were struggling to survive. It motivated me to appreciate everything I love about my city while it's still here— particularly the fun, whimsical aspects, which have inspired the "keep Austin weird" movement.

So one Sunday morning, my daughter and I set out with cameras in hand to document the things that make Austin special. We took picture after picture and put them into a photo album, which became the inspiration for this book.

Today you can share the joy we found in discovering these places. We think you'll be entertained not only by the fun, funky and imaginative landmark art, but also by the stories their creators and owners shared with us. Whether you use the book to take an armchair tour, or as inspiration for your own explorations, we hope you'll enjoy yourself in more ways than you can *Wildly Imagine!!*

photo description: The "Greetings from Austin" mural painted by Skagen & Brakhage is located at Roadhouse Relics, 1720 S. First Street.

ABOUT THE AUTHOR

Vikki Loving

Vikki Loving believes in destiny, true callings and following ones passion. Every human has their own path and Loving has spent decades steering people in the direction of their dreams. After graduating from Sam Houston State University in 1976 with a degree in Criminology and Deviant Human Behavior, she began her career as a recruiter for the Texas Employment Commission and quickly moved up to become Director of Human Resources for such companies as Motorola and McDonnell Douglas. Loving soon realized that she had a gift for matching things.

In 1986, Loving started her own executive recruitment firm, InterSource Executive Search and Contract Solutions (www.intersourcesearch.com), with headquarters in Atlanta. Her expertise, drive and will are evident in the thriving business that at its height had six offices in five states. In 2000, Loving relocated herself and her company's headquarters to Austin.

When Loving returned to Austin from Atlanta in 2000, she and her daughter spent Sundays exploring the city, capturing unique and quirky landmark art with disposable cameras, compiling their treasures in photo albums. Three years later, Loving followed her heart by developing those photographs and experiences into the first book of this series, *Wildly Austin: Austin's Landmark Art.*

Stars of this book are the landmarks that Austinites frequent or pass by every day. They are a part of what makes Austin feel like home to those who live here, and what inspires visitors to return. There will be other books to follow in the *Wildly Austin* series to include *Murals, Architecture* and *Wildly Austin Destinations.*

Loving's pastimes include reading, walking and creating just about anything. She loves to empower others to grow. Her favorite time is any time spent playing with her daughter, writing books together, traveling and discovering the Wildly fun and funky things about Austin and other great cities.

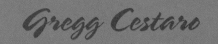

Born in New York City during the sixties; in Asia for a stint as a navy brat; and growing up in Orlando, Florida, Gregg Cestaro has always enjoyed meeting new people and cultures. That is perhaps why he also studied, traveled, and gained both a B.A. and M.A. in Archaeology. For Gregg, art and photography were self-taught. "I have always loved doing detailed illustrations and realism, but fashion editorial and photography is my real passion. I specialize in creative, colorful images of people and situations. In some respects, it is anthropological documentary of local beauty and style. This is especially true for this book where I tried to document Austin's eclectic architecture that will have future value when looking at Austin's past." Living in Austin for five years now, he focuses on photography for the entertainment, modeling, acting, advertising, magazine and science industries. While in Austin he married his best friend of sixteen years, artist Monica Carrell. "Austin is such an incredible place to be— I am so happy to be here!"

CONTENTS
PAGE #

LANDMARK ART

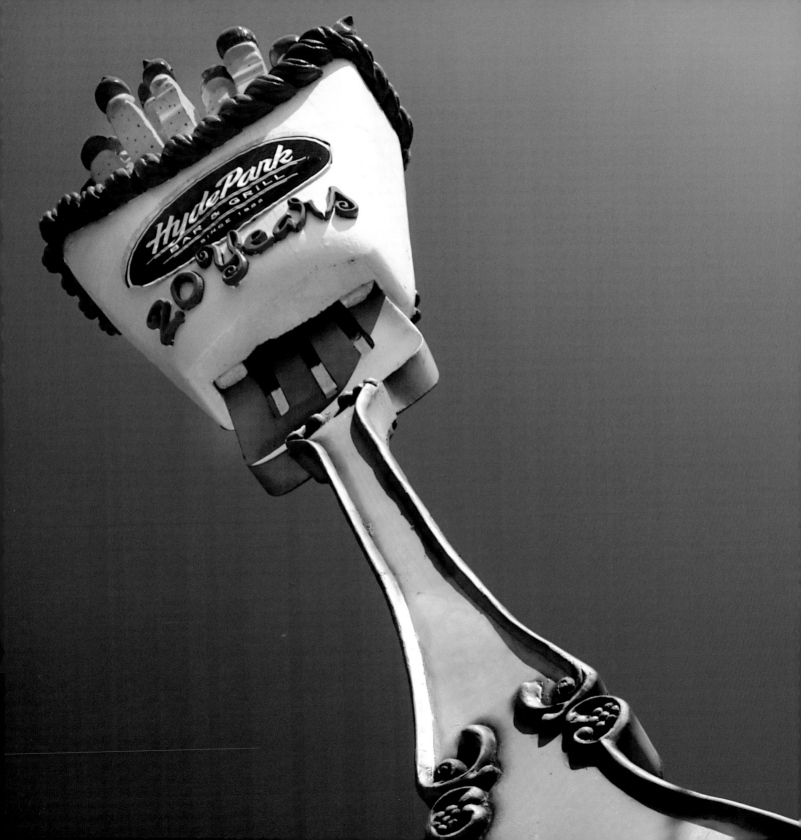

Super-Size It

When Hyde Park residents tell you to "meet me at the fork in the road" for lunch, they're not speaking figuratively.

A 25-foot fork has been standing outside the Hyde Park Bar & Grill since the popular restaurant opened in 1982. Conceived by owner Bick Brown, that fanciful flatware has become a symbol of the Hyde Park neighborhood's quirky charm.

Over the years, a variety of items have perched atop the fork: a giant strawberry (the restaurant's strawberry-topped waffles are a favorite), an Art Deco sandwich, a giant fish, a wedding cake (when Bick got married), a drooping "Dali"-style clock, an eggplant, broccoli (that must have really pulled them in), the earth, and a heart with an arrow for Valentine's. In 2002, the fork held a carton of French fries—their signature item—to mark the passing of the restaurant's twentieth anniversary.

The original fork was designed and installed by artist Richard Heineken. Since then, additions have been made by Dale Whistler and Rich Canter.

HYDE PARK BAR & GRILL
4206 DUVAL STREET
458-3168

 LOCATION MAP 1.

Pumped Up

For more than 20 years, the big, bronze, muscular arm flexing on the side of the Hyde Park Gym has functioned as a kind of urban channel buoy, letting you know you're about to enter one of the more free-spirited areas of Austin. From here, it's just a hop, skip, and jump to that funky thoroughfare known as "The Drag."

Although it serves a broad clientele today, the gym initially catered to hardcore weight lifters. Artist Dale Whistler based his design on original owner Mike Graham's impressive musculature. The veins you see popping out of the Styrofoam and blown fiberglass creation are made from varying sizes of garden hose.

Current owner Dave Goodin says he never has any problem giving directions to his gym — he just mentions the meaty arm on the wall and the usual response is, "Oh, I know where that is." Dave says he agrees with a gym owner visiting from New Jersey, who remarked that the bulging limb "is better than any sign."

It's also more than an advertisement for a local institution. It's an Austin icon that seems to send a message to all: Be strong. Be weird. Be *WILD!*

HYDE PARK GYM
4125 GUADALUPE STREET
459-9174

2 LOCATION MAP 1.

Pizza Monster

Mangia Pizza has the distinction of owning the only vehicular landmark art in Austin. Originally named "Mangia Zilla," the half truck/half creature creation used to roam all over town, amusing everyone it passed and raising the question, "What the heck does a prehistoric monster have to do with pizza?"

"It's simple," says owner Jeff Sayers, "Mangia offers a 'monster' pizza."

Jeff opened Mangia Pizza in 1988 after studying pizza making in Chicago. He was the first to introduce Chicago-style stuffed pizza to Austin. He also created a monster pizza loaded with toppings. The idea for a monster truck soon followed. Mangia Zilla, created by artist Dale Whistler, was put into service in 1989.

Although it was a great advertisement for the restaurant, Mangia Zilla was tough to maintain. Its high-riding noggin was an accident magnet. Drivers were repeatedly warned, but they'd occasionally forget that their dino was too tall to

4

fit in a parking garage causing Mangia Zilla to lose his head more than once. That's why the new delivery truck has the familiar dino painted on. It will also have a new name. It seems that the producers of the 1999 remake of Godzilla feel very proprietary about the use of "zilla," so Jeff is coming up with something less litigious. (Leave it to lawyers to find something litigious about a monster truck.) Although it lacks the magic of the original, the new truck is still pretty cool— cool enough to make a cameo appearance in the Austin-filmed movie, *Cheer Up*, starring Tommy Lee Jones.

Today, you'll find the original truck parked at the Mesa store. The Guadalupe store is under the watchful eye of the 500-pound monster on the roof.

MANGIA PIZZA

8012 MESA DRIVE, 349-2129   **35**   LOCATION MAP 4.

3500 GUADALUPE STREET, 302-5200   **3**   LOCATION MAP 1.

2401 LAKE AUSTIN BLVD., 478-6600   **26**   LOCATION MAP 3.

Up the Creek

One wonders what tragedy befell the broken canoes hanging from the roof of the Waterloo Ice House on 38th Street. Was it an ill-fated trip down perilous rapids? An encounter with Austin's version of the Loch Ness monster? Or did some giant 'gator mistake them for lunch?

Actually, architect Bob Wetmore says his concept was inspired by the famed West Texas Cadillac Ranch, where ten vintage Caddies are buried nose-first in the ground. *Why use canoes?* According to owners Scott Hentschell and Ted Karam, Waterloo was the name of the settlement that later became Austin, and the canoes, which got their weathered look on Town Lake, reflect the initial importance of the city's riverside location.

**WATERLOO ICE HOUSE
1106 W. 38TH STREET
451-5245**

 LOCATION MAP 1.

Mayan Magic

Guatemalan Nobel laureate Miguel Angel Asturias wrote that Guatemala is "a land of natural dreamscapes…mysterious presences and absences."

Having grown up there, American-born Maya Krauss had those same feelings about the Central American country. When she later opened Antigua, specializing in arts and goods from Guatemala, Maya wanted something that would evoke a sense of the country's mystery and magic. She commissioned artist Rory Skagen to design to scale "El Jaguar," an ancient Mayan temple located in Tikal, Guatemala, the largest known Mayan city. Among the last of the great Mayan ruins to be discovered, many consider Tikal one of the most spiritually powerful places in the world.

Although Maya now imports goods from around the globe, El Jaguar remains a fitting icon for a store full of exotic treasures waiting to be discovered.

ANTIGUA
912-1475
1508 S. CONGRESS AVENUE

13 LOCATION MAP 2.

Tough Little Bugger

They say that at the end of the world the only survivors will be cockroaches. In Austin, it'll be cockroaches and the Terminix bug.

The Terminix bug has been hanging around Austin for more than four decades, making it the oldest landmark art in Austin. For a form of life so widely reviled, it has a large following of fond admirers. It's also had a startlingly profound impact on some people. Take artist Todd Sanders, for instance, who did the latest refurbishing of the bug. The former Houston resident said he was just passing through Austin several years ago when he saw the Terminix bug as well as some other great and funky art. Todd "caught" the Austin bug and decided he belonged here.

The beloved bug spent the first 30 years of its life on a pole at the intersection of 12th Street and Lamar Boulevard, where it proved to be a favorite target for fraternity pranks. At first they just tried to ride the pony-size insect. Later, they made several attempts to steal it, succeeding twice.

Then there was the wacky archer who would occasionally shoot the bug with an arrow carrying a note that stated, "Great White Hunter."

The bug was such a fixture at the intersection that it was a shock to long-time residents when Terminix relocated Austin's favorite insect to its new office on Interstate 35. Sadly, when Terminix moved to an office park in 2002, the new landlord had no tolerance for six-legged tenants.

Rather than exterminate their mascot, nicknamed "Willie N. Festus" *(will he infest us)* Terminix created an essay-writing contest to decide who would be its caretaker. The winner was Threadgill's, the Austin institution dedicated to preserving home-cooked food and pre-disco music. It seems Terminix was impressed with Threadgill's record of taking care of other Austin landmarks, like the sign for Hattie's M&M courts, a former brothel on South Congress Avenue.

So all you fans of the Terminix bug can rest easy. Thanks to Threadgill's, Willie will be protecting us from the grackles for years to come.

THREADGILLS SOUTH
301 W. RIVERSIDE DRIVE
472-9304

5 LOCATION MAP 2.

Austin is Batty about Bats

Austin's unofficial mascot is the Mexican free-tailed bat, not just because the city has bats out the wazoo, but because the furry, winged creatures are so weird they're cool. Naturally, these unique mammals chose a bridge on South Congress to "hang," where they'd feel right at home with the eclectic eccentrics of SoCo. The bats like Austin so much that they've created the largest urban bat colony in North America, reaching 1.5 million occupants at peak season.

To honor the bats, the Downtown Austin Alliance commissioned artist Dale Whistler to craft the 18-foot-tall bat sculpture that's located at the intersection of South Congress Avenue and Barton Springs Road. It's near the spot where people gather at dusk from mid-March to early November to watch the bats take off in pursuit of their evening meal. It's a sight to behold, making the bats one of the top five tourist attractions in the capital city.

**SOUTH CONGRESS AVENUE AND
BARTON SPRINGS ROAD**

6 LOCATION MAP 2.

Golf Course and "Sculpture Garden"

When Glen Dismukes built things in his spare time, he didn't just putter around. His labors of love are the defining feature of Peter Pan Miniature Golf, which has provided family entertainment at the intersection of Barton Springs Road and South Lamar Avenue for more than half a century. As you putt your way through the course, you'll encounter amongst Glen's masterpieces— a towering Tyrannosaurus rex, a pirate, a pig, a turtle, and, of course, Peter Pan.

Glen took over the family-owned business in the early 1970s. Glen's son and current manager, Mike, fondly recalls how his father spent hours in the garage behind his Venetian blind store, crafting creatures out of metal frames and masonry concrete. Glen's biggest project, the dinosaur, was created with sprayed foam and fiberglass when he was 75.

Looking at the whimsical sculptures going up around town today, it appears Glen was ahead of his time.

PETER PAN GOLF
1207 BARTON SPRINGS ROAD
472-1033

7 LOCATION MAP 2.

A Knight in Shining Patio Armor

The Saxon Pub and "Old Rusty," the knight standing guard in front of the popular club, have something in common—they've both withstood the test of time. The knight in "patio armor" has been standing guard since owner Joe Ables opened the club in 1989. Like the music featured in the 1960s-style music club, Old Rusty is an original— how often do you see a medieval knight crafted out of old lawn chairs?

Many an act has passed before Old Rusty's unblinking gaze. The club started out as a songwriters' place, featuring the likes of Stephen Fromholz, Michael Martin Murphy, and Rusty Wier. Today the offerings have broadened to include something for everybody. If you're lucky, you might even be around when stellar musicians like Bonnie Raitt and Kris Kristofferson drop in.

Yep, Old Rusty's heard quite a bit from his post outside the Saxon Pub, and to many loyal patrons, the sight of that tall, funky knight evokes memories of great music and good times. Let's hope Old Rusty never rusts out.

SAXON PUB
1320 S. LAMAR BOULEVARD
448-2552

8   LOCATION MAP 2.

Taco Goddess

Arms raised heavenward, the Taco Goddess seems to be suggesting that salvation awaits within Taco Xpress — salvation for anyone weary of assembly-line Tex-Mex and yearning for the real deal. Or perhaps she's dancing to the music that frequently rocks the little establishment. Or maybe she just wants to give you a big hug.

If you know owner Maria Scorbalan, all three are possible.

A former resident of Argentina and Mexico, Maria endured a long, frequently harrowing journey before finding success on South Lamar. She started her taco business in 1996 in a trailer on a lot next to the current restaurant. The tacos were a hit from the start, but word didn't really get out until music was added to the menu, thanks to gratis performances by the likes of Alejandro Escovedo and other local musicians. Today, Taco Xpress is one of the hottest spots in town for Sunday Gospel brunch.

Regulars will tell you it's also one of the friendliest restaurants in town. That fun, feel-good atmosphere is reflected in the frequent changes in the Taco Goddess's garb. Whether she's in a boa, a wedding dress, or a Halloween costume, the lady with the outstretched arms (a likeness of Maria doing her best Eva Peron imitation) is sending a message: Stop here to fill your stomach and warm your soul.

TACO XPRESS
2529 SOUTH LAMAR BLVD.
444-0261

 LOCATION MAP 2.

Definitely NOT Chicken Little

Did you ever feel like you needed a mother hen to watch over you? If so, you should probably move in with Austin artist Faith Shexnayder — she has the mother of all mother hens standing guard in her yard.

According to Faith, her oversized hen is a cocky, rule-the-roost kind of bird. Faith sees the work of art as an embodiment of the mother hen attitude, telling people: "Don't mess with my chicks." And you know what they say: When a five-foot tall chicken tells you something, you'd better listen.

But this bird is actually more than just a work of art. Faith designed it to be part of her children's playground. It's sturdy enough to hold active kids and has gentle curves that make it suitable for climbing.

If you're in the neighborhood, come check out our favorite hen. Just don't tell Colonel Sanders.

RESIDENCE
708 WEST GIBSON STREET

18 LOCATION MAP 2.

Fitting Tribute

When first sighting the metal globe above South Lamar Boulevard, your initial impression might be that it's advertising a travel agency. Nope, it's about being free-spirited rather than foot-loose. Owner Jane Clarke named her vintage clothing shop Amelia's Retro-Vogue & Relics to honor the famous aviator Amelia Earhart, whom she said, "had the rules her way."

A metalsmith by training, Jane convinced artist Evan Voyles to let her participate in making this landmark piece six years ago. While Evan constructed the ribs of the eight-foot-high world, Jane pounded the continents into shape and determined which cities would be illuminated with electric lights — you can't miss Austin.

The finishing touch was the plane, modeled after Amelia's Electra 10E. With the magic of neon, Evan set the plane in perpetual motion around the globe, symbolizing both the lingering impact of Amelia's contributions and the mystery of her disappearance.

AMELIA'S RETRO-VOGUE & RELICS
2024 SOUTH LAMAR BOULEVARD
442-4446

10 LOCATION MAP 2.

Hi-Ho Jackalope

Like most of the things at Uncommon Objects, the jackalope above the front door made a long and interesting journey to the South Congress antique store.

Co-owner Steve Wiman says the fiberglass critter was rescued from a Dallas landfill by his sister-in-law. Back then it was a bunny rabbit. Steve put it in his front yard in Dallas, but eventually some cranky neighbors asked him to remove it. Steve figured that the oversized cottontail would make a perfect sign for his new store, Uncommon Objects, which he opened in Austin.

When Uncommon Objects moved just down the street a few years after its opening, Steve brainstormed with Austin artist Evan Voyles about doing something a little more interesting with the bunny. Inspiration came from the vintage Texas postcards that feature a cowboy on the back of a jackalope. Evan elongated the rabbit's ears, added pink eyes, constructed a cowboy out of a muffler and a tail pipe, and added a neon lariat. The result was a perfect advertisement for the kind of funky, unusual items in the store.

The jackalope inspired other store owners to add whimsical 3-D art and off-beat features to their storefronts, contributing to the unique feel of SoCo.

UNCOMMON OBJECTS
1512 SOUTH CONGRESS AVENUE
442-4000

14 LOCATION MAP 2.

Rockin' Burgers

Remember Kip's Big Boy, the chubby, smiling, ten-foot pre-adolescent who invited diners into Big Boy Restaurants across the country? The figure above Fran's Hamburgers could pass for his slimmer, hipper sister. In fact, her name is Big Girl.

The retro hamburger queen created by the clever guys at Blue Genie Art Industries is a perfect match for the popular eatery, which is stuck in a time warp. The restaurant opened in the early 1970s, a period that many consider Austin's "Golden Age."

Why the guitar? Well, many of the restaurant's patrons are musicians, and owner Ed Terrazo wanted to honor those folks and all the performers who labor in the Live Music Capital of the World. So next time you're on South Congress, cruise into the comfortably worn drive-in and enjoy what many consider to be the best burger in town. Who knows? Maybe Big Girl will play a few tunes while you eat.

FRAN'S HAMBURGERS
1822 SOUTH CONGRESS AVENUE
444-5738

15 LOCATION MAP 2

Texas-Sized Rooster

Poultry tycoon Frank Perdue once said, "It takes a tough man to make a tender chicken." So what kind of man makes a really, really big chicken? An artist with an Austin sensibility of course.

The Rooster, which creator Todd Sanders fondly refers to as the "Poor Man's Peacock," was originally commissioned by a customer. The plans called for the bird to be six feet from beak to tail, but during carving it grew to be nine feet long. The customer couldn't use that big a bird so Todd kept it and delivered a smaller copy to the customer. Todd put the Rooster up on his roof, and since a big bird has a big appetite, he added a mammoth worm, emerging from a nearby wall, for the Rooster to feast on.

The Rooster has many publicity credits to include having been featured on Russell Crowe's music video. Take a look at page 63 to see Todd riding him bareback. Now that is a real Texas ride!

ROADHOUSE RELICS
1720 S. 1ST. STREET
442-6366

17 LOCATION MAP 2.

Serengeti Samba

What do you get when you cross a 1940s musical with an episode of Wild Kingdom? Well, it just might be a giant zebra dressed as Carmen Miranda—complete with a fruit basket headdress. That's exactly what sits atop the roof of Austin's most unusual costume store, Lucy in Disguise With Diamonds.

Jenna Radtke opened two stores, side by side, on April Fool's Day in 1984. Lucy in Disguise With Diamonds, with zebra stripe décor, offered eclectic costumes. Electric Ladyland, painted in wildly vivid colors, sold vintage clothing. Eventually the costume business overwhelmed the vintage clothes, and the two stores merged — as did their diverse decorative themes.

The zebra made its debut in 2001, courtesy of the artisans at Blue Genie, and its festive look blends perfectly with the carnival atmosphere in the store. The zebra has no official name, but Jenna, with a grasp of both puns and pop culture, often refers to her as Carmen Zebra Jones.

**LUCY IN DISGUISE WITH DIAMONDS
1506 SOUTH CONGRESS AVENUE
444-2002**

12 LOCATION MAP 2.

Chillin' in South Austin

You know, if Don Powell's experience is anything to go by, a snowball's chance in Austin might not be all that bad. For the past 11 years, Don and his wife have run Sno Beach, a snow cone stand and a South Austin institution. In addition to delicious servings of shaved ice and syrup, the Powells also dish up a heaping helping of Austin charm, courtesy of the Snow Cone Man, the giant snow cone in shades that sits atop their stand.

Don got into the snow cone business after retiring from a career in cotton farming and cattle ranching. It was Mrs. Powell who suggested they open a snow cone stand. Don quickly purchased the stand and all the equipment.

Needing a little advertising help, Don decided he would find something to draw attention to his business. Enter the guys at Blue Genie. They took a giant statue of a snow cone (grape…yum) and added an oversized pair of shades to give the creation a bit of attitude. Thus, the Snow Cone Man was born. For those who tend to miss the obvious, it says "Cool" right on the front of the giant cone. But we don't think the Snow Cone Man needs much help getting that message across.

SNO BEACH
302 SOUTH LAMAR BLVD.

 LOCATION MAP 2.

Largemouth Bass Eats Hula Hut!

It looks like it's lunging for an unwary diner on the open-air deck of the Hula Hut — but this giant bass wouldn't even hurt a hydrilla (that nasty, propeller-fowling plant that plagues Lake Austin).

The steel and fiberglass fish was rescued from its perch atop a restaurant in Dallas (talk about a fish out of water!) and given a more fitting, aqueous home near Lake Austin's Tom Miller Dam, where it could truly be appreciated.

It's not only cool to look at—it does tricks, too. Feed it quarters, and it'll spew water. (The money goes to charity.) However, management asks that you don't feed it anything else —the mannequin some nut stuffed in its jaws was particularly hard to extricate.

Owner Michael Young, a co-owner of the Chuy's chain, likes to include art in most of his restaurants because he believes that "art enhances people's lives." We agree, and you'll feel even more enhanced if you view it from the deck with a frozen margarita. Cheers to artist Bob Wade.

HULA HUT
3826 LAKE AUSTIN BLVD.
476-4852

 19 LOCATION MAP 3.

You May Get
an Eyeful at
Austin's Eiffel

The 21-foot model of the Eiffel Tower outside Dreyfus Antiques is the only piece of landmark art that wasn't created in the United States — owner George Dreyfus bought it in France. But it fits into the Austin scene just fine, thank you.

There's something about that miniature French icon that brings out the goofiness in people. Here are some classic examples: the guy in a King Kong suit who had to be removed from the tower…the young woman who took off her bathing suit top to have her picture taken with the structure…the occasional college kid snapped while reclining on a couch in front of it. And on three occasions, romantically inclined men have inquired about using the site for a Valentine's Day picnic. One guy even brought a table, complete with linen tablecloth and candles, and placed it directly under the tower.

That's what we like about Austin: If you supply the place, someone else will bring the party.

DREYFUS ANTIQUES
1901 N. LAMAR BLVD.
473-2443

23 LOCATION MAP 3.

Tiptoe to the Tulip

Although it may never rival our love of the bluebonnet, we Austinites have also developed a fondness for the tulip. Well, at least one tulip. Specifically, the gigantic flower that towers over Prima Dora, an eclectic gift boutique located on South Congress.

Diana Prechter opened Prima Dora in 2000 in an old 7-11 building. How Austin is that? She originally planned to sell flowers and hats, so she commissioned the giant tulip to draw attention to her business. Unfortunately, her deal with her flower supplier fell through and she abandoned that part of the plan. The tulip, however, stayed. As did the attention it generated.

Prima Dora now sells gifts and jewelry and plenty of hats in the shadow of the giant tulip. If you're in the neighborhood, tiptoe over and check it out.

PRIMA DORA
1912 SOUTH CONGRESS AVENUE
447-4736

 LOCATION MAP 2.

Big Footprint

The boot hanging outside 1614 Lavaca St. gets the prize as the most understated landmark sign in town. Its simplicity belies the fame and rich tradition of the business within.

Capitol Saddlery has been operating at that address for more than 60 years, and its bootmakers have carved a reputation as craftsmen of exceptional quality. Celebrated country singer Jerry Jeff Walker wrote an ode to Charlie Dunn, the bootmaker who put Capitol Saddlery on the map. That star-quality craftsmanship, carried on by Charlie's protégé, Ramon Navarro, has been sought after by celebrities, politicians, high-profile musicians, and ordinary folk in the market for extraordinary boots. In our opinion, when you don a pair of boots from Capitol Saddlery, you're *wearing* landmark art.

CAPITOL SADDLERY
1614 LAVACA STREET
478-9309

20 LOCATION MAP 3.

CAPITOL *Saddlery*
LUGGAGE REPAIR
BOOTS
SADDLES

SHOE REPAIRS

Watch Out When You Hear Him Rattle

We can't say for certain, but the 80-foot rattlesnake slithering around Ranch 616 may be the longest herpetological sculpture on the planet. Conceived by artist and Texana aficionado Bob Wade, the big 'ol rattler was inspired by the South Texas Ice House theme of the downtown restaurant. The giant reptile was even constructed from assorted junk one might find lying around a ranch. For instance, fabricator Evan Voyle used a pitchfork for the tongue, rain gutter material for the body, and fog lights from an old truck for the eyes.

The snake started out on paper as an 8- to 10-foot creation for the bar. But as the idea coiled around Bob Wade's fertile mind, it grew into the monster you see today. Bob just wanted to remind everybody that in Texas, we do things big.

RANCH 616
616 NUECES STREET
479-7616

Go Saints!

There's no mistaking who the owners of Shoal Creek Saloon are backing when pro football season rolls around. You could probably fit half of the New Orleans Saints offensive line in the gleaming football helmet on the saloon's roof. Whenever the Saints are playing, you can be sure the venerable watering hole is rockin'. Saints fans come from surrounding counties to join the lively crowd gathered around the big-screen TV and enjoy a plate of Cajun food, along with the camaraderie.

The Saint-centric tradition was born out of necessity. Die-hard Saints fan Bud George used to drive from bar to bar with like-minded buddies, asking the managers to please put on the Saints game. Ray Canfield, Shoal Creek's owner, answered their plea. Bud enjoyed Sundays there so much that he eventually became the manager of Shoal Creek Saloon and helped transition the place into a New Orleans Saints sanctuary complete with authentic Cajun food.

So check it out the next time the Saints are playing. Even if you're not a Saints fan, it's an excuse for a good ol' New Orleans'-style party.

SHOAL CREEK SALOON
909 N. LAMAR BLVD.
474-0805

 LOCATION MAP 3.

Greening Loves Red

People get attached to their pets — but a Longhorn? It's that bond between man and beast that led to the creation of the longhorn statue in front of the Greening Law Firm at 506 W. 15th Street.

It happened like this: Just for the heck of it, Attorney Ron Greening bid on a live Longhorn at a charity auction. Danged if he didn't win. Now what? Luckily, he was in the process of moving into a new home out on Lake Travis, a three-acre spread previously owned by famed oil well firefighter Red Adair. Ron named his new pet "Red" after Red Adair and turned him loose. Welcome home big fellah!

Ron soon got so attached to the hulking bovine that he hated to drive off to work each morning and leave him behind. He decided he needed a life-sized Longhorn at work that resembled Red. So he hired artist Dennis Ford to sculpt his design of a12-inch high then an 18-inch-high version of the Longhorn. After Dennis was comfortable with those, Ron convinced him to go — all the way to life size. The resulting wonder of the Longhorn world stands proudly in front of Ron's office.

GREENING LAW FIRM, P.C.
506 W. 15TH STREET
476-0888

 **24** LOCATION MAP 3.

Fashion Gorilla

El Jefé, a concrete gorilla serving as Clarksville yard art, seems to have more outfits than Cher. The gorilla changes clothes to match the seasons, the holidays, or the whim of its owners, Dr. Jim and Mrs. Liz Fox.

Familiar costumes include a red thong and heart for Valentine's Day, a yellow jersey and bike for the celebration of Lance Armstrong's win in the Tour de France, and a Santa beard and cap for Christmas.

El Jefé has been a celebration of silliness ever since the fun-loving couple brought him home to fill an empty space in their yard. It started with a well-attended unveiling party, complete with Vienna sausages, screw-top wine, and Cheetos. Since then the famous gorilla has received marriage proposals (we assume these love-struck suitors were in an altered state), offerings of bananas, and love letters. It just goes to show: give Austinites something slightly wacky and they go ape.

**EL JEFÉ
710 WEST LYNN STREET**

25 LOCATION MAP 3.

Skullopus

Here's a uniquely Austin recipe: Start with a giant skull, complete with death's head grin. Place it atop the body of an octopus and cap it all off with a pirate's hat. What do you get? Something that's going to sell a lot of tattoos, apparently.

Skullopus, the oddly named mascot of Atomic Tattoo, has been glowering ominously over the Burnet Road store since 1997. Owner Larry Edwards was actually on his way to pick up a neon sign for his business when he stumbled into the Blue Genie workshop and saw a large skull under construction. He asked about purchasing it, and the next thing you know — well actually after a long, creative process that we won't even try to describe — they had decided to combine the skull with the octopus body and pirate hat. And, thus, Skullopus was born.

Unusual? You bet. Different? No question. But in Austin, unusual and different are good marketing strategies, and even after all these years Atomic Tattoo's Burnet Road location, with Skullopus watching over it, does more business than the other stores. Could it be that Skullopus is responsible? We wouldn't bet against it.

ATOMIC TATTOO
5533 BURNET ROAD
458-9693

Atlas Shrugged

Do you think the owners of Chuy's felt like they could hold the weight of the world on their shoulders when they put Atlas outside their restaurant at North Highway 183 and Duval? Well…possibly, since Chuy's was already a beloved Austin institution by that point. Chances are they were also looking to inject a little "South Austin charm" into that corner of the city.

The statue, the heart of which is a copy of the famous work from New York's Rockefeller Center, began its life outside a gym in Dallas. But they say everyone in Texas wants to move to Austin and apparently statues are no different. Local artist Evan Voyles purchased Atlas and brought him to town, where the architect building the new Chuy's saw it and decided he had to have it for the restaurant.

Of course, most things coming from Dallas need funking up to make it in Austin. So Voyles added fins atop the globe to spell out "Chuy's" and a flying saucer base constructed out of satellite dishes covered in Mexican mirror globes. And then he put the whole thing on a rotating pedestal. Let's just say it's hard to miss it from the highway.

Tragedy of tragedies — all that hard work almost went to waste. One night Atlas shrugged. When workers arrived in the morning they found the globe, with Atlas's hands still attached, lying on the ground. Fortunately, after hours of emergency artwork, the hands were reattached to the body, the globe reinstalled, and Atlas stands head, hands, and shoulders above the streets of northwest Austin.

CHUY'S RESTAURANT
11680 N. RESEARCH BLVD.
342-0011

34 LOCATION MAP 4.

49

Security Guards

It's not every day that a wife receives a pair of seven-foot-tall mythological beasts as a surprise gift from her husband. But to Kathy Halbert, who co-owns Halbert Antiques with her husband Mike, the twin griffins were a perfect present.

The Halberts had recently moved into their new store at 5453 Burnet Road, and things just weren't the same without a couple of griffins around. Smaller versions of the winged lions had decorated the posts of the gated entrance to their previous location, and people had used them as landmarks to find the store.

For the new location, artist Faith Schexnayder sculpted two griffins holding a torch between them — an appropriate symbol for a husband-and-wife business team. Also fitting, which the antique dealers later discovered, is the role of griffins in Greek mythology. They're the guardians of the treasures of the world.

Judging by the size of the beasts, the treasures in the store are well protected.

HALBERT ANTIQUES
5453 BURNET ROAD
451-8037

Bright Idea

Lightbulb Shop owner Edwin McGary came up with a clever way to simplify directions to his little specialty store: "Just go north on Burnet from Koenig Lane and look for the 18-foot-tall Lightbulb Man." (Hint: He resembles Conan O'Brien, the towering, red-headed, baby-faced host of the late-night talk show bearing his name.)

Edwin's lightbulb business was strictly wholesale until 1986, when he decided to open a small retail shop in front. He hired the imaginative crew at Blue Genie to create the Lightbulb Man because he wanted to bring some of South Austin's funky art north of the river. The art has been featured in Entrepreneur, Business Success, and The Franchiser magazines and has drawn inquiries and letters from all over the world.

It just proves that even when you're small, it pays to think big.

**LIGHTBULB SHOP
6318 BURNET ROAD
453-2852**

 LOCATION MAP 4.

Two-Headed Longhorn Turns Heads

No, the County Line on the Hill isn't promoting a two-for-one special with its two-headed longhorn outside the restaurant. It's just there for a hoot. "We take our food and service seriously but not much else," says Marketing Director Scott Ziskovsky.

Scott and cohort Skeeter Miller, County Line's owner and Director of Operations, bought the Bob Wade creation during the contentious 2000 presidential election, so they named their oddity "Neck and Neck." They first installed it at their San Antonio restaurant. It attracted plenty of attention, but nothing like the night they moved it to Austin.

As Scott tells it, they were hauling the life-size bovine in a trailer when, somewhere between San Marcos and Austin, they noticed the trailer was no longer behind them. (We're not saying this is why it happened, but Scott and Skeeter have been known to hoist a few.) In a panic, they turned around and tore back down Interstate 35 in search of their beloved beast.

Not long afterward, they caught the attention of an alert DPS officer. When the officer pulled them over and asked, "What's the rush?" Scott said they were looking for a two-headed longhorn in a wayward trailer. The officer just shook his head. He said he'd already hauled in three drivers to be tested for DWI who said they were speeding to get a second look at a two-headed longhorn tooling up the interstate.

Scott assured him that the freakish critter was indeed theirs and asked for his assistance. The officer agreed to help (imagine that initial conversation with his dispatcher), and they soon found the stray in a ditch near Buda.

Today "Neck and Neck" makes frequent but unscheduled appearances outside the restaurant. Scott and Skeeter don't dare leave it outside permanently — it's too tempting to cattle rustlers.

COUNTY LINE ON THE HILL
6500 W. BEE CAVES ROAD
327-1742

 LOCATION MAP 5.

Fabulous Flamingo Flock

Austin's famous flock of flamingos has been brightening the intersection at Highway 360 and Bee Caves Road since 1989. The colorful gathering began when Pots and Plants owner Pat Swanson placed two birds on the grassy slope in front of his place and sold them before he could even get back inside. So more flamingos were put out, followed by others, then still more... When he was through, Pat had turned ordinary yard art into an Austin landmark.

Most people who drive past appreciate the sheer whimsy of the scene. Even President Bill Clinton had to buy a pair of birds when he was in town. However, there was a point in time when these faux flamingos were an endangered species.

It could be said that the first battle to "Keep Austin Weird" was fought over those gloriously goofy birds. It seems that at one point the 'powers that be' in Westlake considered the birds a blight on the upscale community and sought to have them removed. Other Westlakers were up in arms over the prospect of losing the flock. The battle drew correspondents from the Associated Press, United Press International, CNN, and National Public Radio, and even Jay Leno joked about the brouhaha on the Tonight Show. In the end, the pro-flamingo crowd won, and the Pots and Plants lawn became a sanctuary for the beloved birds, reminding us that free spirits still prevail in Austin. Don't forget to look for the penguins that come to the lawn in August; it is reported that they come in an effort to coax the cold fronts in from the North!

POTS AND PLANTS
590 BEE CAVES ROAD
327-4564

 LOCATION MAP 5.

I Dream of Genie

This blue genie doesn't come out of a lamp, doesn't sound like Robin Williams in a Disney flick, and doesn't grant wishes— unless of course you're wishing for a distinctive, eye-catching piece of artwork for your home or business. The guys at Blue Genie Art Industries seem to grant that wish regularly.

Blue Genie got its start in the late 1990s when a group of Austin artists, including Rory Skagen, Dana Younger, and Kevin Collins, decided to disband their separate businesses and join forces. After collaborating for many years on a variety of artistic adventures, they decided they needed a way to take on larger projects that used all their diverse skills. So they founded Blue Genie Art, naming their new company after a statue they had lying around the workshop. How's that for recycling?

You don't have to go far in this town to encounter the creative genius of the artists at Blue Genie. The guitar-toting "Big Girl" at Fran's Hamburgers, the Aztec Ruin at Antigua, the Zebra at Lucy in Disguise, Skullopus at Atomic Tattoo, and the Light Bulb Man at the Light Bulb Shop all testify to the brilliant teamwork by the guys at Blue Genie. And the satisfaction of another wish fulfilled...

BLUE GENIE ART INDUSTRIES
916 SPRINGDALE ROAD
444-6655

 LOCATION MAP 6.

WELCOME

God Bless America

If you find yourself lost in East Austin, there's a handy map you can check on Martin Luther King Blvd. But the scale might be a little large. The giant concrete map of the United States in Ira Poole's front yard has been a neighborhood fixture for almost three decades, along with its companion, a replica of the Statue of Liberty.

In the early 1970s, Mr. Poole's front lawn looked pretty much like everyone else's. But as the U.S. bicentennial approached, Mr. Poole — a dedicated teacher with a passion for the U.S. Constitution — felt the need to create a tribute to his country. A former student told him about a copy of the Statue of Liberty being sold in Dallas. Mr. Poole skipped his vacation that year, shelled out $1,000 for the statue, and lugged it down to Austin. And that was the beginning of something big.

With the lady ensconced on the lawn, Poole turned to building his map, fashioning a mold out of plywood and rope and pouring the concrete himself. His project generated so much interest that a neighbor loaned him workers to move the finished map into place.

Over the years, Ira's collection has grown to include the U.S. and Texas flags and a large star fashioned out of native Texas stone. If you stop by Mr. Poole's house for a look, make sure you sign his guest book — you'll see that Austin's own local patriot has attracted visitors from all over the world!

RESIDENCE
2400 E. MARTIN LUTHER KING BLVD.

30 LOCATION MAP 6.

About the Artists

BLUE GENIE ARTISTS

One of Blue Genie's earliest clients proclaimed owners Rory Skagen, Dana Younger, and Kevin Collins "gods of 3-D art." That might be a little over the top, but it's an example of the kind of adulation Blue Genie generates. We might go so far as to call them the lords of Austin's 3-D art, because more than any other artists, their imaginative 3-D sculptures have helped give SoCo its unique vibe.

FROM LEFT TO RIGHT: **DANA YOUNGER, KEVIN COLLINS, IAN SHULTS, RORY SKAGEN, AND CHRIS COAKLEY.**

The guitar-toting "Big Girl" atop Fran's Hamburgers, the wacky yet stylish zebra in Carmen Miranda garb above Lucy's in Disguise, Antigua's Mayan temple, and the long-lashed dragon at Dragon Puffs were all created by Blue Genie's artists. Several other works are scattered around town, ranging from murals to bas-reliefs.

Blue Genie was formed in 1999 and takes its name from Rory's first successful foam sculpture, which lords over the neighborhood from the roof of the company's East Austin studio. The guys say they've flourished, in part, because of the symbiotic relationship between artists and Austin. After all, where else would you find a strip like South Congress where people are willing to display the kind of whimsical sculptures Blue Genie creates? Says Dana Younger, "There's a quality to what we produce that's specifically Austin."

BLUE GENIE ART INDUSTRIES
916 SPRINGDALE ROAD
444-6655
RS@BLUEGENIEART.COM

TODD SANDERS

Would you ever move someplace because you saw a giant insect? Lured to Austin in 1997 by the giant Terminex bug (which he later refurbished) Todd Sanders set up Roadhouse Relics in a dilapidated storefront in South Austin and started producing the art he loved: vintage metal and neon signs reminiscent of the 1930s and 1940s.

You can find Todd's work all over Austin. Roadhouse created the big clock at the original Threadgill's restaurant on Lamar, the collection of neon signs in Threadgill's south location, and the Mercury Man at the Continental Club. Todd also helped renovate the State Theatre.

But most Austinites know Todd because of Roadhouse's funky headquarters on South First Street. The property sports such eye-catching scenery as a massive mural of a "Welcome to Austin" postcard, the word "Austin" in huge, red neon letters atop the backyard trailer where Todd lives and of course our favorite, the giant rooster with a big appetite going after the worm.

ROADHOUSE RELICS
1720 S. FIRST STREET
442-6366
WWW.ROADHOUSERELICS.COM

Photo by hkphotograpy.net

EVAN VOYLES

You probably know Evan Voyles' work, even though you may not know him. Evan may have contributed more to Austin's colorful nighttime glow than any other artist in town. The luminous art he produces through his company, Neon Jungle, is some of the most recognizable in town.

A former Buda antique dealer, Voyles got into the sign business in the mid-1990s when his shop burned down  and all that remained were the vintage signs out back. Evan still has a passion for old things (some would call it junk), which he uses to perform artistic alchemy, turning scrap metal and other refuse into works of art.

Among the works on his resume are Chuy's Atlas, the globe above Amelia's Retro-Vogue and Relics, the Alamo Drafhouse tower, the snake at Ranch 616, and the jackalope-riding cowboy at Uncommon Objects.

NEON JUNGLE
2026 S. LAMAR BLVD.
680-0809

FAITH SCHEXNAYDER

 Artist, designer, and sculptor Faith Shexnayder loves what she does. A third generation painter from a long line of artists, this native Austinite dreamed of being an artist since childhood. And she's made that dream a reality.

Faith's whimsical and engaging works can be seen all over town. We especially like the magical Griffins outside Halbert Antiques on Burnet Road and the giant Mother Hen that stands in her front yard watching over her "chicks."

In her own tour de force, she even designed a float to carry local hero Lance Armstrong in a Tour de France victory parade. Despite the prominence of her works, Faith keeps her business low-key. She does little advertising and gets most of her business through word of mouth. Of course, having Lance for a reference probably doesn't hurt.

FAITH SCHEXNAYDER
448-2256
SCHEX@AUSTIN.RR.COM

BOB "DADDY-O" WADE

It's a good thing Bob Wade is a native Austinite because if he wasn't, we'd have to adopt him. Any guy nicknamed "Daddy-O" who pulls around an Iguanamobile and creates works of art like a two-headed longhorn is clearly a product of Austin's quirky, creative environs. The Fort Worth Star-Telegram called him a "pioneer of Texas Funk and connoisseur of Southwestern kitsch." We'd agree.

Bob mines the old West and the Texas depicted in vintage photographs and postcards for inspiration. His best known works include the 40-foot-tall cowboy boots parked at a San Antonio shopping mall, and the giant iguana that used to reside on the roof of the Lone Star Café in New York. A better kept secret is his serious work, which includes the 25-foot longhorns in the Alumni Center at the University of Texas.

BOB WADE, WWW.BOBWADE.COM

DALE WHISTLER

Dale Whistler is the grandfather of Austin landmark art. The former ad agency artist created two of Austin's oldest and most recognized sculptures — the muscular arm at Hyde Park Gym and the giant fork in front of Hyde Park Grill. He also proved that his mojo is still working by producing one of Austin's most recent landmarks: the bat at the south end of the Congress Avenue Bridge. The rotating bat was voted Austin's favorite outdoor sculpture in an *Austin Chronicle* poll.

Long-time Austin residents were also quite fond of Dale's Mangia Zilla, Mangia Pizza's monster delivery truck (now retired). And who wouldn't want to adopt the dog and cat Dale created for the Town Lake Animal Center on West Cesar Chavez Street.

Dale's work enlivens interior spaces, too. Check out his eye-catching mobiles at the Austin Children's Museum and the Whole Foods store at the Gateway shopping center.

Today, Dale lives in Norway (a woman lured him there, wouldn't you know it?). But he'll never really be "gone." With all the great work he left behind, a part of Dale will always be right here in Austin.

DALE WHISTLER, KRISTINEANDDALE@C2I.NET

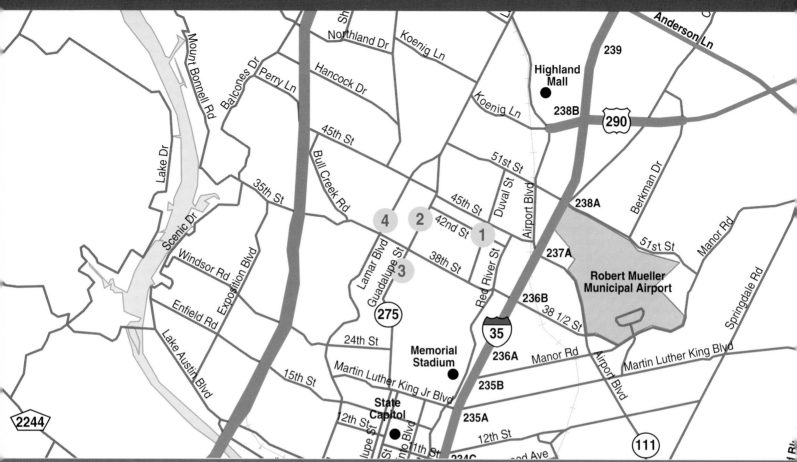

Hyde Park & University

1	**Fork**	Hyde Park Bar and Grill, 4206 Duval St.
2	**Arm & Barbell**	Hyde Park Gym, 4125 Guadalupe St.
3	**Monster**	Mangia Pizza, 3500 Guadalupe St.
4	**Canoes**	Waterloo Ice House, 1106 W. 38th St.

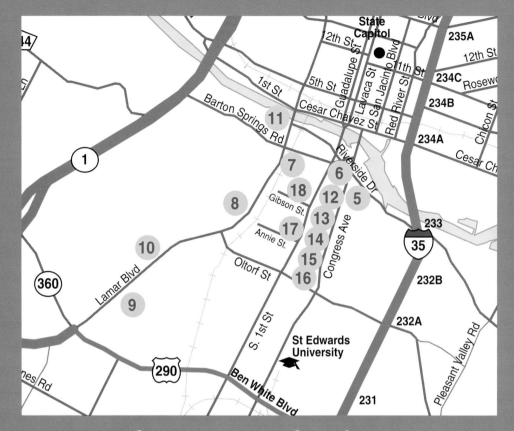

South Congress & South Lamar

5	**Terminix Bug**	Threadgills South, 301 W. Riverside Dr.
6	**Bat**	S. Congress Ave. at Barton Springs Rd.
7	**Dinosaur & Peter Pan**	Peter Pan Golf, 1207 Barton Springs Rd.
8	**Suit of Armor**	Saxon Pub, 1320 S. Lamar Blvd.
9	**Woman**	Taco Xpress, 2529 S. Lamar Blvd.
10	**Globe and Airplane**	Ameila's Retro, 2024 S. Lamar Blvd.
11	**Sno-Cone**	Sno Beach, 302 S. Lamar Blvd.
12	**Zebra**	Lucy in Disguise, 1506 S. Congress Ave.
13	**Mayan Ruins**	Antigua, 1508 S. Congress Ave.
14	**Jack-a-lope**	Uncommon Objects, 1512 S. Congress Ave.
15	**Girl with Guitar**	Fran's Hamburgers, 1822 S. Congress Ave.
16	**Tulip**	Prima Dora, 1912 S. Congress Ave.
17	**Rooster & Worm & Greetings Austin Mural**	Roadhouse Relics, 1720 S. 1st Street
18	**Chicken**	Residence, 708 W. Gibson St.

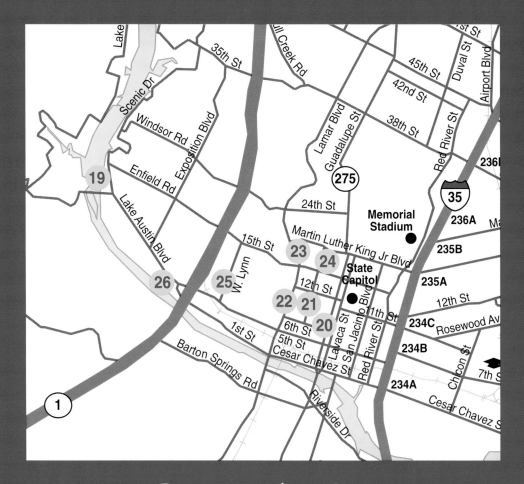

Downtown & Lake Austin

19	**Fish**	Hula Hut, 3826 Lake Austin Blvd.
20	**Boot**	Capitol Saddlery, 1614 Lavaca St.
21	**Snake**	Ranch 616, 616 Nueces St.
22	**Football Helmet**	Shoal Creek Saloon, 909 N. Lamar Blvd.
23	**Eiffel Tower**	Dreyfus Antiques, 1901 N. Lamar Blvd.
24	**Longhorn**	Greening Law Firm, 506 W. 15th St.
25	**Gorilla**	Residence, 710 West Lynn St.
26	**Mangia Truck**	Mangia Pizza, 2401 Lake Austin Blvd.

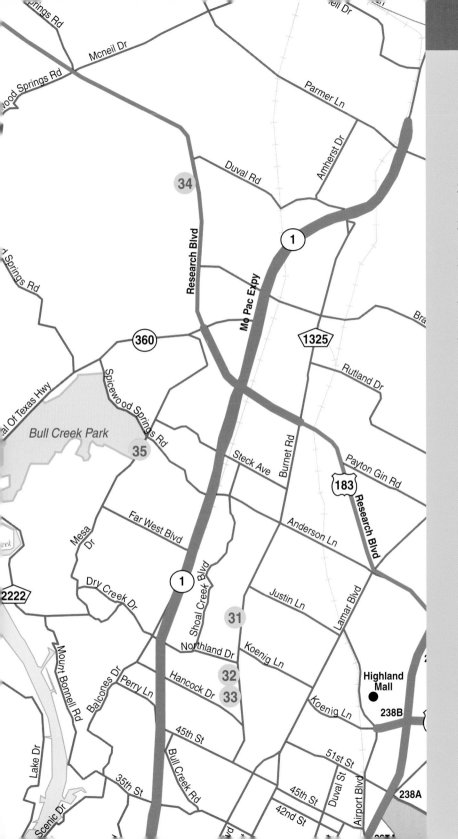

Central / North

31 Light Bulb Man
Light Bulb Shop, 6318 Burnet Rd.

32 Skullopus
Atomic Tattoo, 5533 Burnet Rd.

33 Griffins
Halbert Antiques, 5453 Burnet Rd.

34 Atlas
Chuys, 11680 N. Research Blvd.

35 Monster Truck
Mangia Pizza, 8012 Mesa Dr.

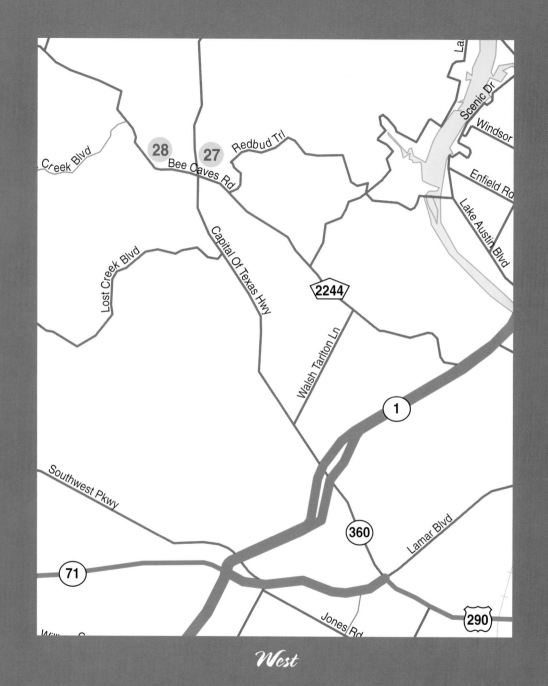

West

27 **Flamingos**　　　　　　　Pots and Plants, 5902 Bee Caves Rd.
28 **Two-Headed Longhorn**　County Line on the Hill, 6500 W. Bee Caves Rd.

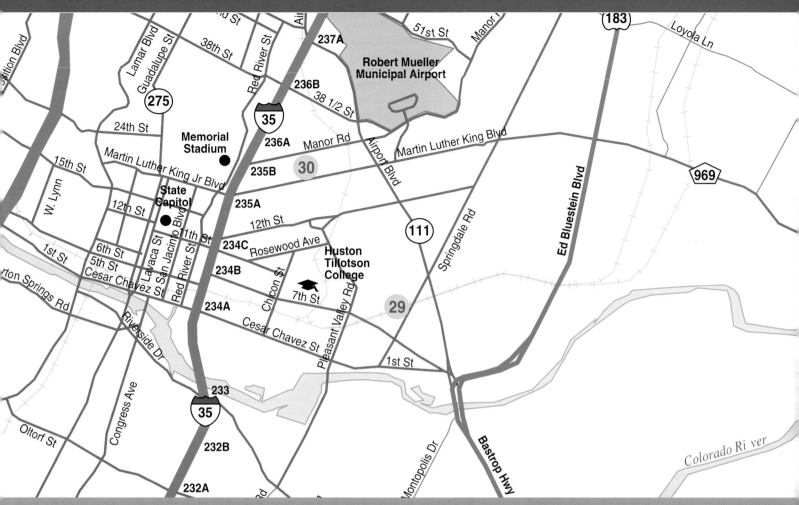

East

29	**Blue Genie**	Blue Genie Art, 916 Springdale Rd.
30	**Statue of Liberty & Map**	2400 Martin Luther King Dr.

Wildly Austin Press specializes in publishing unique books about Austin, Texas. It is our hope that you've enjoyed this first book of the "Wildly Austin Series" and look forward to our future titles.

WE WELCOME YOUR IDEAS FOR ANYTHING YOU FEEL IS
"WILDLY AUSTIN." EMAIL SUGGESTIONS TO: VIKKI@WILDLYAUSTIN.COM

Wildly Austin Press

For more information about our other titles or to order additional copies of this book please contact:

WILDLY AUSTIN PRESS
P.O. BOX 161987, AUSTIN, TEXAS 78714-1987
WWW.WILDLYAUSTIN.COM